SPELL FOR MELTING ICE

Still in love with London where she has lived almost all of her quite long life (born 1945), **Kate B Hall** writes and reads a lot and belongs to a couple of poetry groups, gets published occasionally in anthologies and haiku magazines, received The British Haiku Society Museum of Haiku Literature Award, May 2021. Kate has published two Haiku collections, *Running for nothing* (Ram 2004) and *Irises* (Hub 2015). She edited *Show of Hands* (2016), a collection of poems by Blue Side Poets. Her first poetry collection, *The Story Is* was published by Bad Betty in 2018. She is at present working on a collection of sonnets. She has the most lovely family and lives with her life partner in West London near the Thames.

Spell for Melting Ice

Published by Bad Betty Press in 2021
www.badbettypress.com

All rights reserved

Kate B Hall has asserted her right to be identified as the author of this work in accordance with Section 77 of the Copyright, Designs and Patents Act of 1988.

Cover design by Amy Acre

Printed and bound in the United Kingdom

A CIP record of this book is available from the British Library.

ISBN: 978-1-913268-19-0

Spell for Melting Ice

PRESS

Spell for Melting Ice

*In memory of my son Rory and my sister Di,
who both brought me so much joy.*

Contents

Before There Was Deoderant	9
Instead of Snow	10
The Ring	11
Persiflage	12
This Man	13
Coniston	14
Spell for Melting Ice	15
1965	16
Sister	17
The Don and I	18
All the Things You Are	19
Visiting My Sister in Penzance, Cornwall	20
Slower	21
The Bed You Died In	22
Yellow Plastic	23
my chant against death	24
Acknowledgements	25

Before There Was Deoderant

Tonsillitis making me
restless at night,
I was allowed to have
my mother's petticoat,
when she took it off for bed.
Tucked in next to me,
held to my cheek
still warm from her body.
Silky soft, soothing,
the smell of eau de cologne
and a hint of perspiration.
More comforting
than she could ever be.

Instead of Snow

A mist covered land, warm and steamy.
I watch as a sheep drowns, its unshorn sodden wool
drags it down, it struggles and bleats as it sinks,
I can see its plight but I am floating too far above it.
I wonder where I am, as I stare at familiar landmarks.
I know it's winter, still I take my jacket off,
it falls slowly and is held on the surface of the water.
An exhausted crow, one of my favourite birds, lands on it,
its weight causes a sudden sinking, engulfing
the struggling bird, that cannot get the purchase to rise,
still flapping, it sinks and drowns.
The next day a child asks me why we don't have
much snow any more, I try to explain.
She complains that she doesn't like the rain.

The Ring

Supposing I die in a sinking ship,
lose my wedding ring. My hope would be
that you were with me and lost yours too.
We'd be eaten by the fish and our rings
would fall off our bones to the bottom.
Or what about I swim across the big bay?
That would be quite an achievement.

A diver found a ring on the sea bed,
there was no shipwreck near it.
A plain silver band, traditional for rings
exchanged during marriages, years ago.

The diver went to the maritime museum,
discovered a hundred years before
a woman marathon swimmer, who was
seventy-five years old, had crossed the bay.
She broke all previous records
but lost her wedding ring on the way.
Her wife was proud and happy she was safe
and of course the wedding ring was replaced.

Persiflage

A fancy name for an unkind joke,
the stab of confusion at four years old,
he finds a place to hide until tea time
when all is forgotten. Boys must be
toughened up because they will be teased,
bullied, ridiculed. Slowly he learns
to laugh it off and as he gets older
to banter and backchat. Later when sarcasm
slips effortlessly from his tongue,
he feels proud, in spite of a lingering sting.
He thinks he was loved, that it was just part
of growing up, it certainly did him no harm.
His anger can be dangerous.

This Man

He appeared on the TV
old now, much older than me.
When I was thirteen and fourteen
I didn't know it wasn't OK,
still I didn't tell anybody.
It was thrilling, made me feel grown up
when he pulled me behind
a curtain or into the bathroom,
pressing against me, his hands
inside my clothes. I didn't struggle,
I thought he liked me, wanted me
but this man never asked me out,
never brought me flowers.
Later I felt ashamed of the pleasure
but eventually began to understand,
so when he appeared on the screen
it was rage alone that gripped me.

Coniston

The walk there was hard, a long flat
path over rocks by Coniston Water
until the soles of your feet bruised.
Then up a path steep and wild
to the summit of not-quite mountain.
The path flattened and there:
the glint of golden water.
A tarn to lie down with
and rest, soothed by
the green of the grass,
warmed by the sun.

A place to remember long after
and to dream of,
even though you can no longer
make the climb.

Spell for Melting Ice

Take from the earth
cold elements, cast them
into a vessel
shiny and hard.

Mix ancient trees
black and unsustainable
with soft metal,
heat until they sizzle.

To aid your magic
you may chant
I don't care, I don't care
I don't care.

1965

Running with the pram up Liverpool Road,
shouts follow us, our son is asleep.
It is late and dark. His father has the pram,
my high heels mean I struggle to keep up.
The drunks get bored, go back to the pub
still laughing and shouting n*****.
Calling me a dirty slag. Back home
we are both shaking, terrified.

Outside the butchers in Holloway Road
two women lean over his pram.
His father gets there first. His colour
confirms, as they have been loudly
discussing, that the baby is a little darkie,
Can I touch his hair, for luck?   No!

Sister

Night in a dark room waiting for the morning light.
An eternity, cold air even here inside.
I shut my eyes against the icy wind that creeps
under the door. Then the night steals
me back, pulling me under water, where
you and I hold hands one last time.

We leave the sea, cars fill the carpark,
we run and run on the sand, followed
by your black cat from years ago.
I wake up, warm and in my own bed.
I know I should get on with my life,
that it is time to let you go but I don't
even though you have no idea who I am.

The Don and I

One November evening, after nursery school, my mother,
my sister and I went to Islington Central Library.
I found, in the adult section, what seemed to me,
to be the biggest and most beautiful book in the world.
The brown leather cover, deeply embossed with gold,
inside there were bright pictures of a strange man
on a very old donkey by a broken down windmill.
I slipped this treasure into my mother's shopping bag.

Surprisingly, given the book's weight, my mother
didn't notice it until after tea. The next evening
I was marched back to the library, made to give the book back
and to apologise for stealing, my first public humiliation.
That Christmas I was given a children's version of the book
Don Quixote, my first hero, who dared to dream.

All the Things You Are

Inspired by a Lemn Sissay workshop

You're
my new sight now the cataracts are gone,
the old jacket I get out when it gets cold,
the glass of wine with my birthday dinner,
the poem I wrote that was rather bold.

You're
my favourite book made into a film,
the fountain pen I got to save plastic,
the plants I sometimes forget to water,
my worries at night that may be fantastic.

You're
a vegan cake in my favourite café,
the berries and seeds the birds come to eat,
the sun coming out when the sky is grey,
how glad I am that I live in this street.

You're
the pride I feel overflowing like the wind,
walking home at night with a bag of chips,
that uplifting feeling when a plane takes off,
the songs we sang that are still on my lips.

Visiting My Sister in Penzance, Cornwall

The last time I saw my sister in her own home
she looked suspiciously at me when she opened the door.
I said, *Hello Lovely Sister*, she stepped back to let me in.
We watched rugby on the television which was constantly on.
Oh look, she laughed, *those little boys are pushing each other over.*
We fell asleep after lunch, my coughing woke her
Oh Kate she said, remembering her smoking sister
from long ago then the moment was gone. She slept until I left.

It doesn't snow much in South West Cornwall
but it did the next day. Quite naturally she went out to look.
She slipped and broke her ankle, a neighbour found her
on the pavement, called an ambulance.
I was cut off in St Ives, her daughter in Flushing.
Taken to hospital, she never went home again.

Slower

Now most of the people I know
walk faster than me
their legs have grown longer
their lungs bigger than mine.
You and I used to go for long walks
but now we don't match
so in the interest of compromise
we don't go so far
and when the path is narrow
forcing single file
you mostly walk at the back
so I don't get left behind.
Often I feel feeble old and sick
like next door's dog.
If I say anything everyone says
don't be silly and *it's fine*
but it isn't and sometimes
I just want to be left behind.

The Bed You Died In

I take the bed that you died in
and drag it into the sea.
It floats at first, the mattress
helps but the metal is too heavy
for a raft and slowly it sinks.
Taking my memories of you
tucked up snug and warm.

Nothing is lost, simply changed,
by the sea. On the seabed below
the mattress and covers
slowly decay and disintegrate.
The frame of the bed will be left
like a shipwreck, a skeleton.
You belong more in the sea
than the crematorium.

Yellow Plastic

The irony all those years ago
of bright yellow, plastic daffodils
that came free with modern detergent.
They sat cheerful as anything
on my friend's mother's mantelpiece.

My mother hated plastic flowers,
said they were common.
She didn't think much of my friend's mother either
but I rescued our daffodils from the bin
and took them to her anyway.

my chant against death
After Mervyn Morris

remember cancer
remember hospital
remember visitors
remember cannulas

remember partner
children
growing up grandchildren
crying

remember books
writing
Mozart's music
country walks
picnics

remember don't
remember stay

Acknowledgements

Many thanks to Amy Acre, Jake Wild Hall and Liz Evans for all their support, suggestions and love. Plus my excellent Stanza Group who have contributed to my poetry over some years, and who will recognise some of these poems. And all the tutors I have attended classes and workshops with, who have all been pretty wonderful.

www.ingramcontent.com/pod-product-compliance
Lightning Source LLC
Chambersburg PA
CBHW021455080526
44588CB00009B/865